Blank Comic Book

130 pages 8.5 x 11

Various templates to create your own comics

By Vitaliy Lyen and Orange Cat

This book belongs to

____

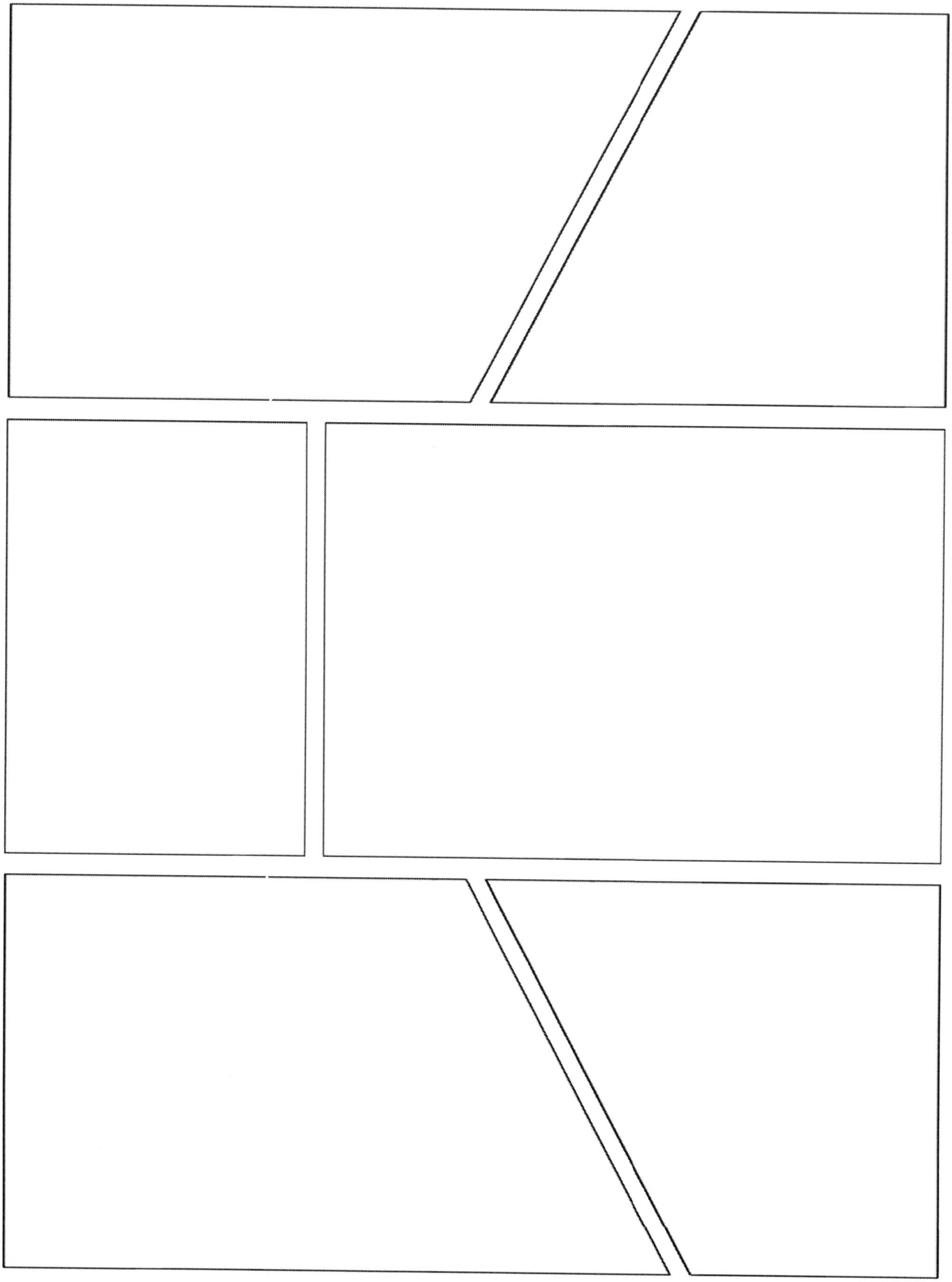

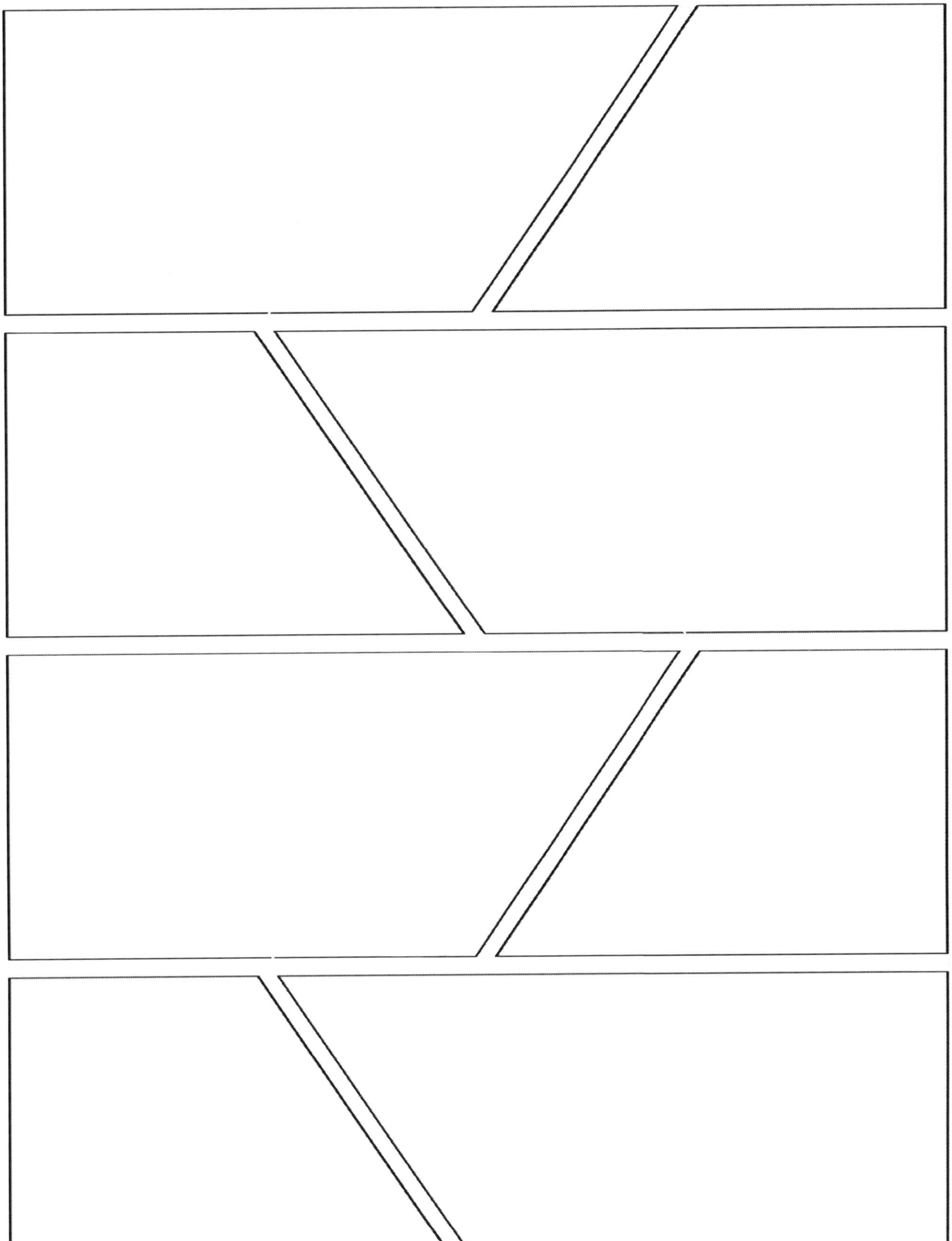

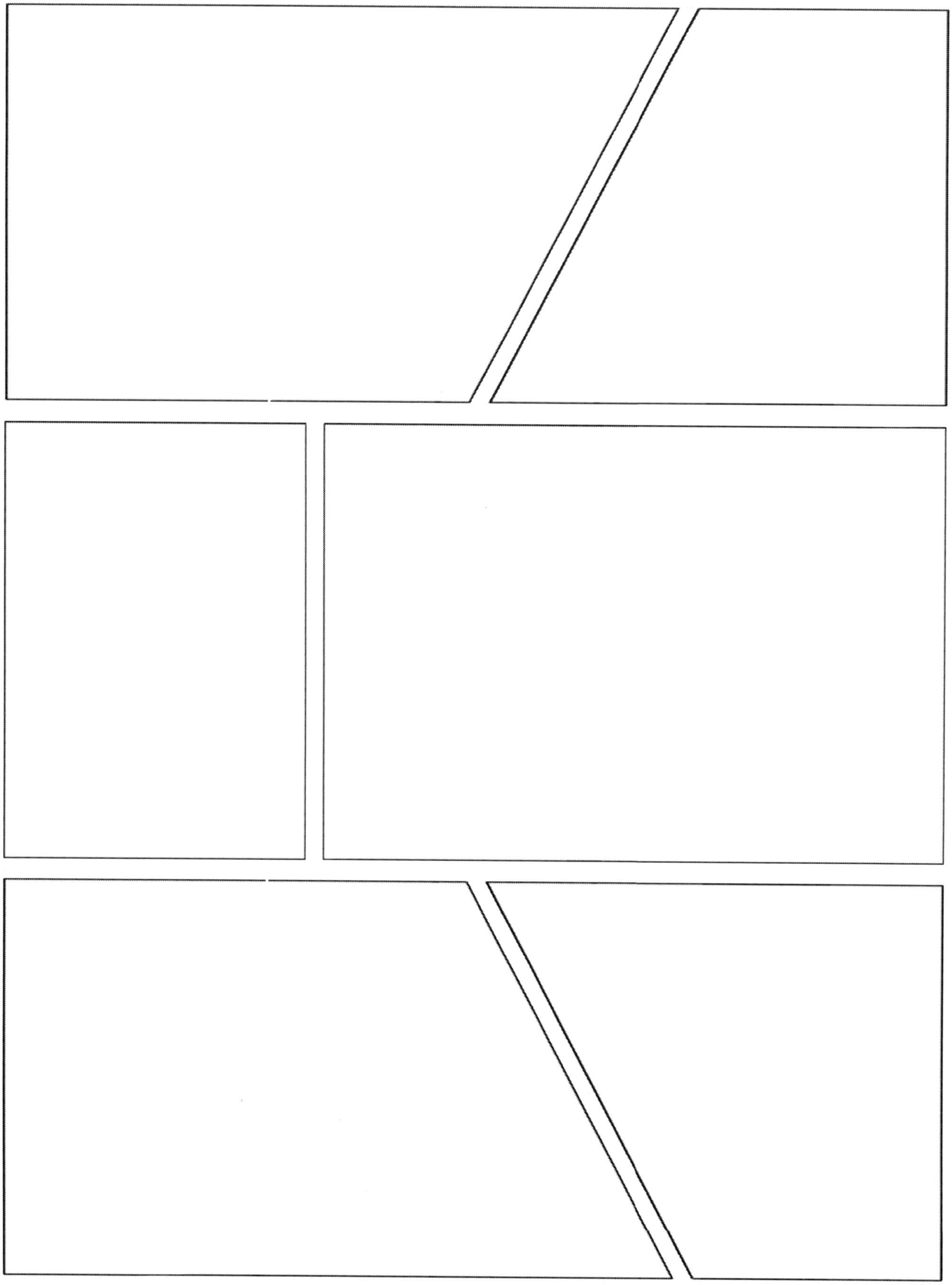

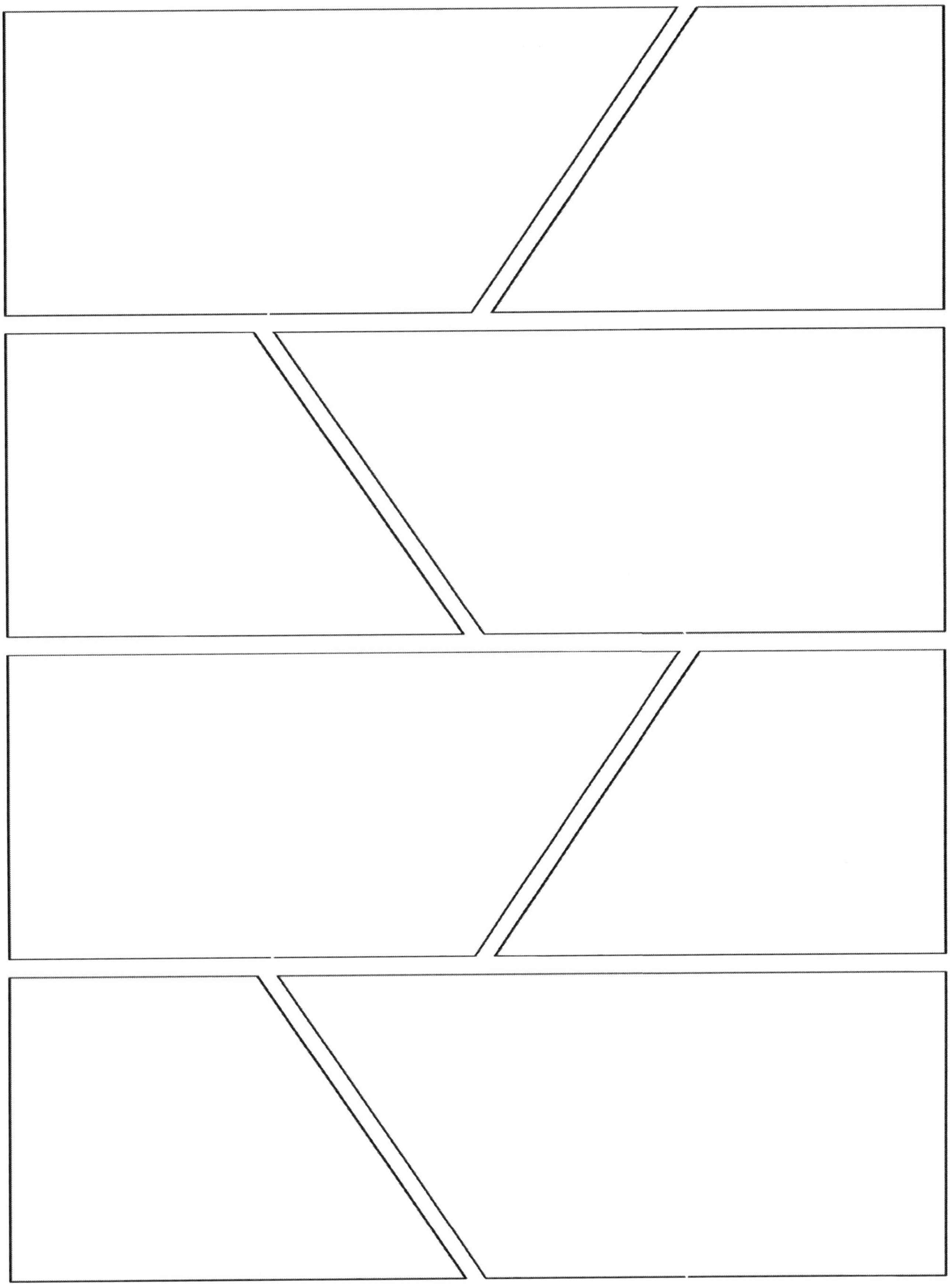

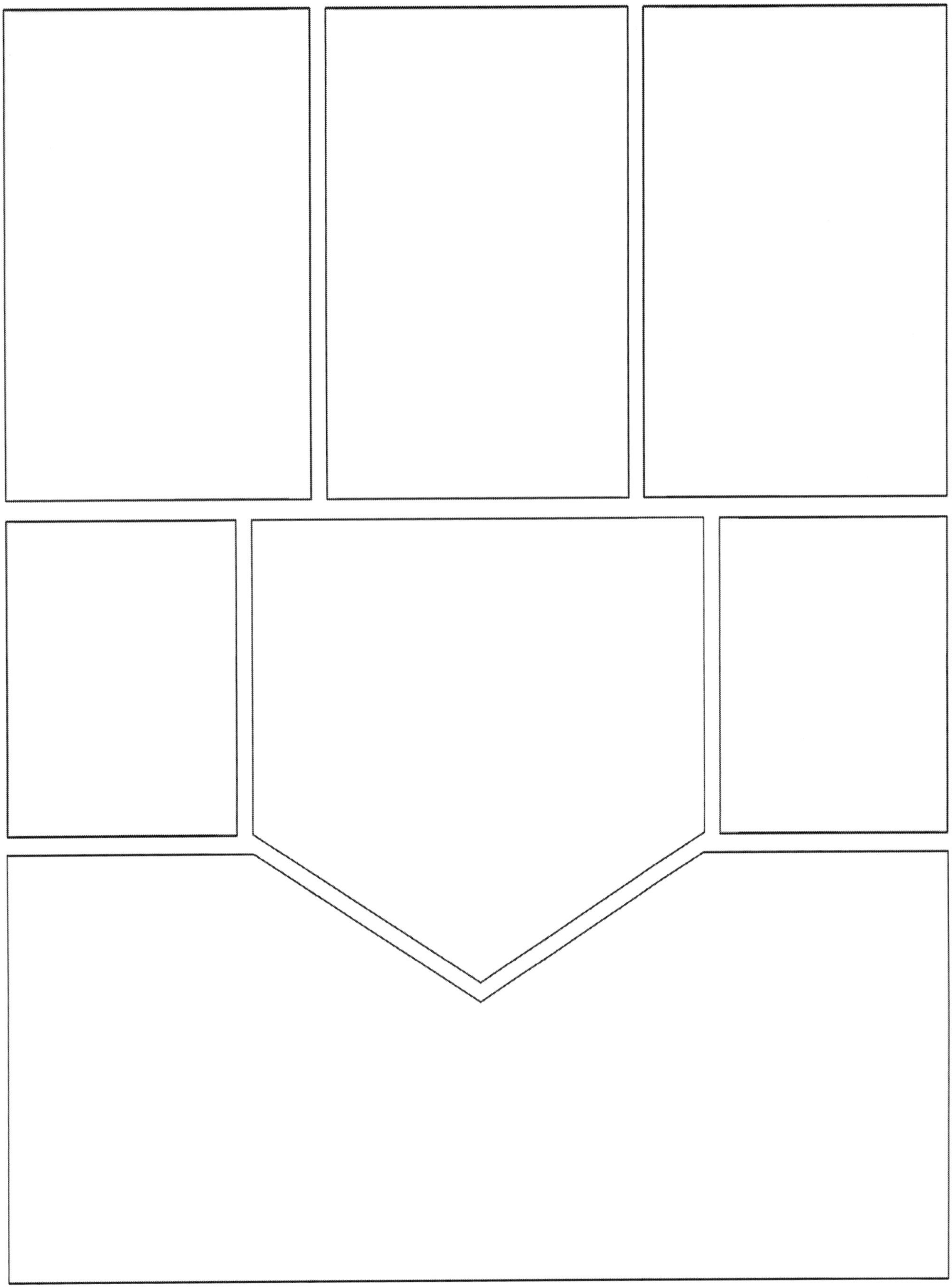

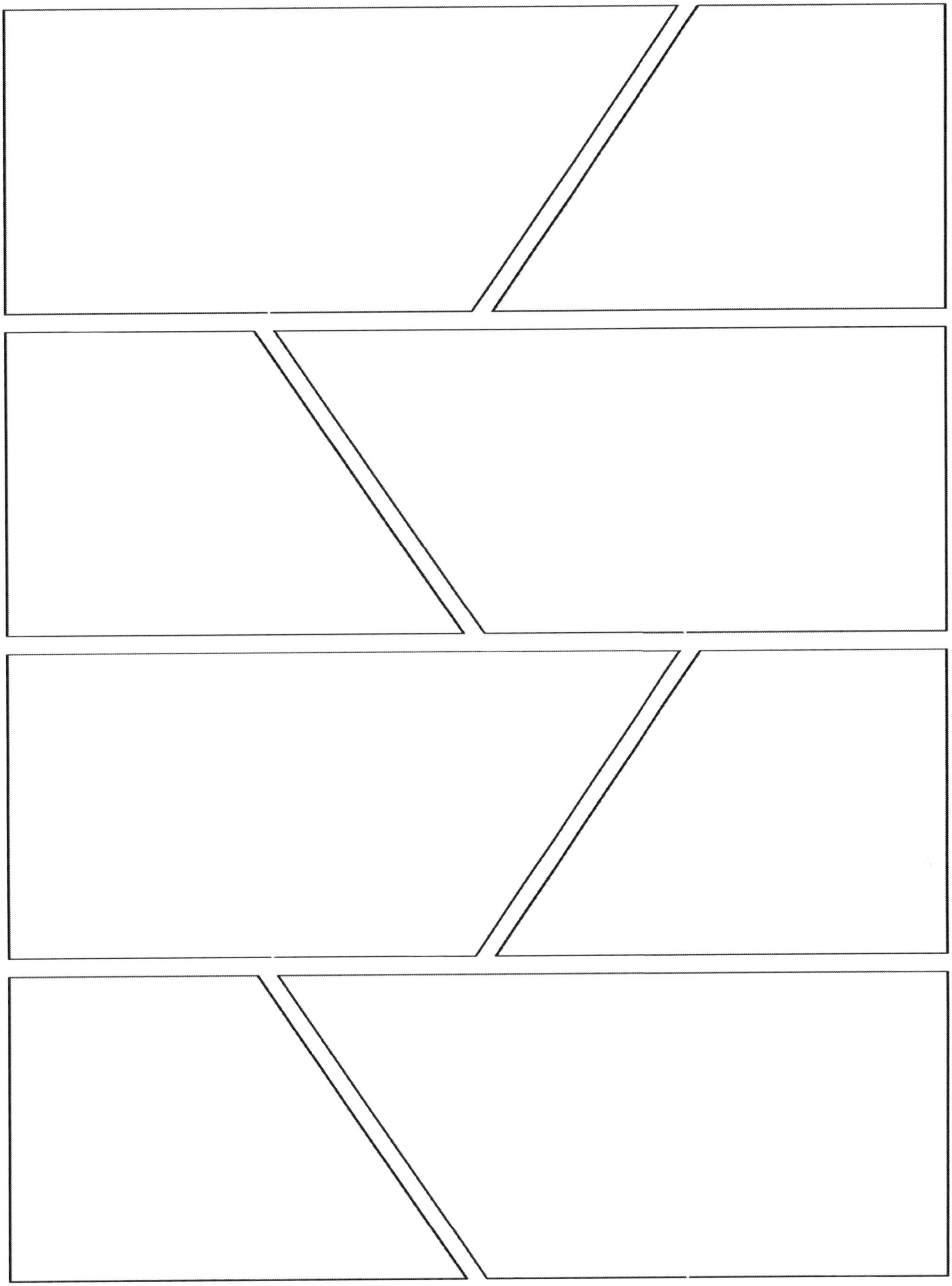

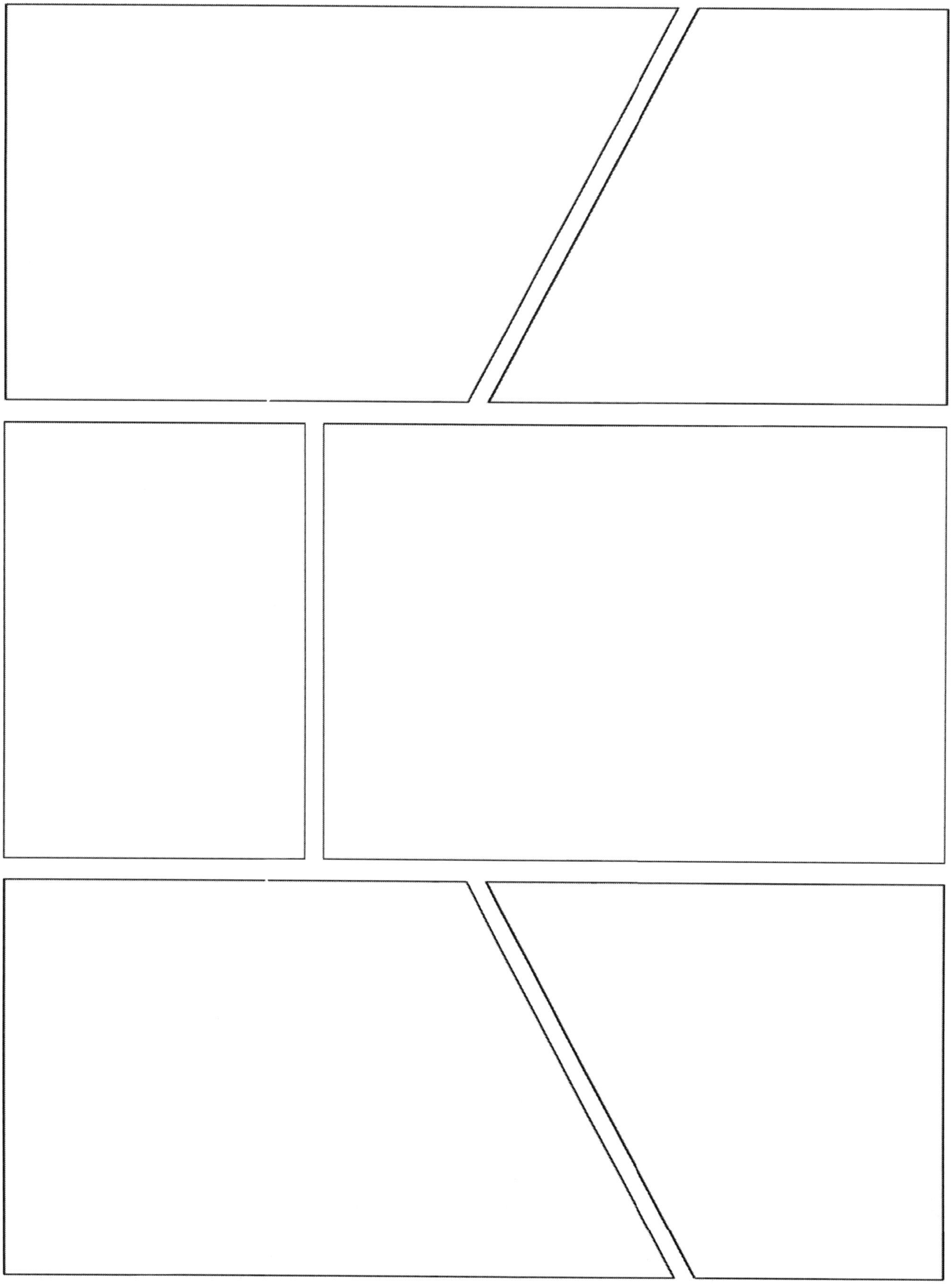

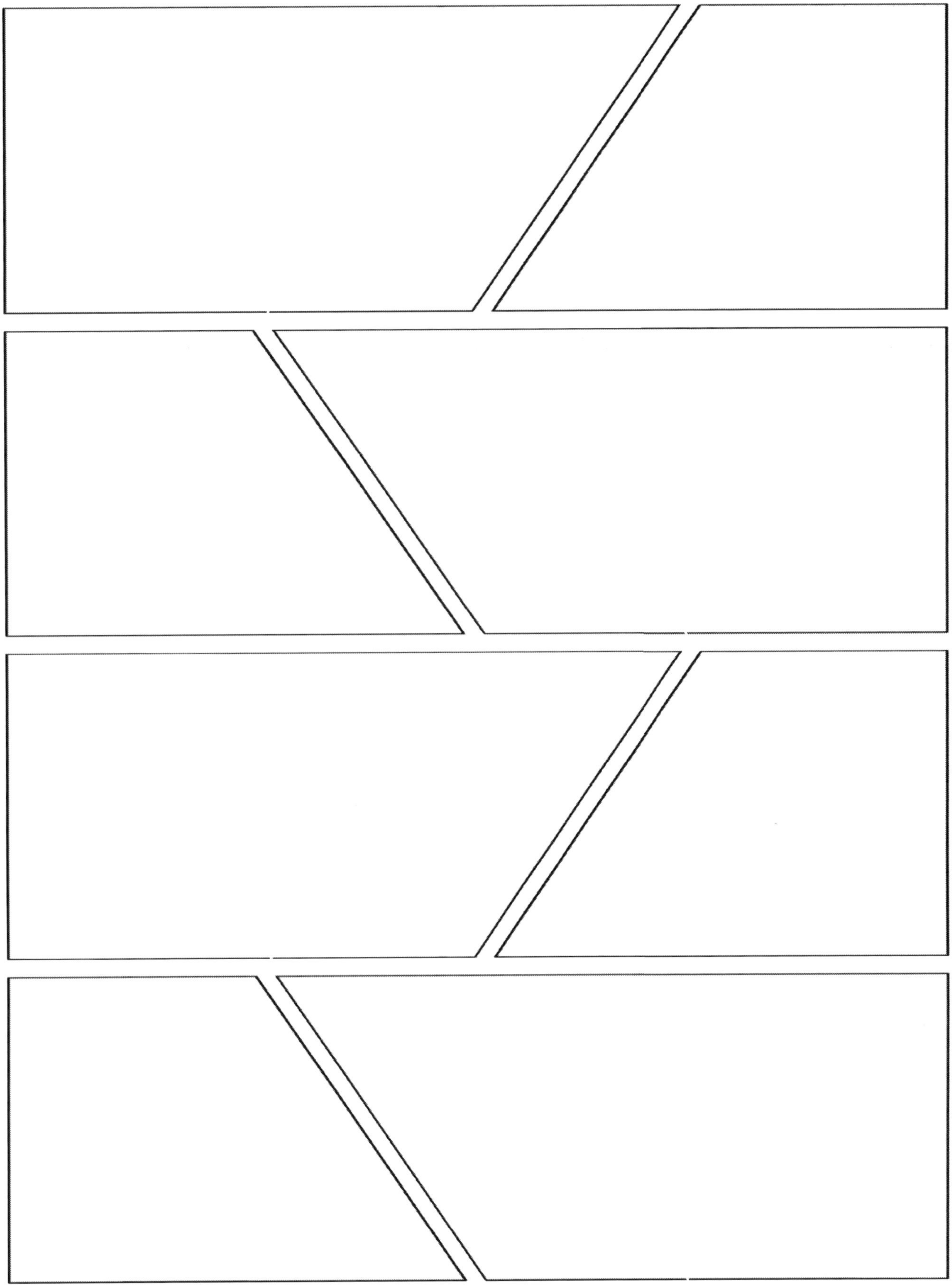

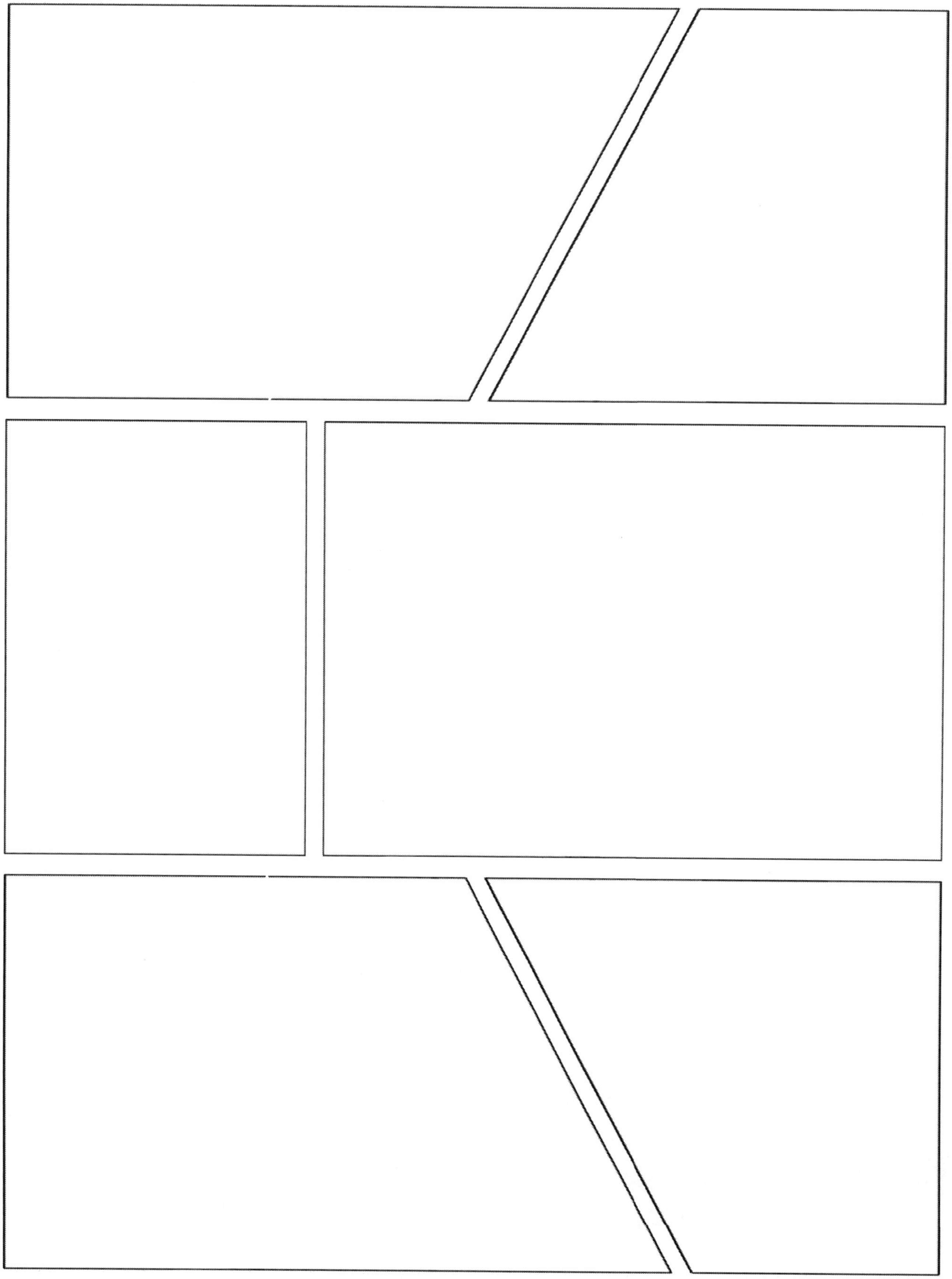

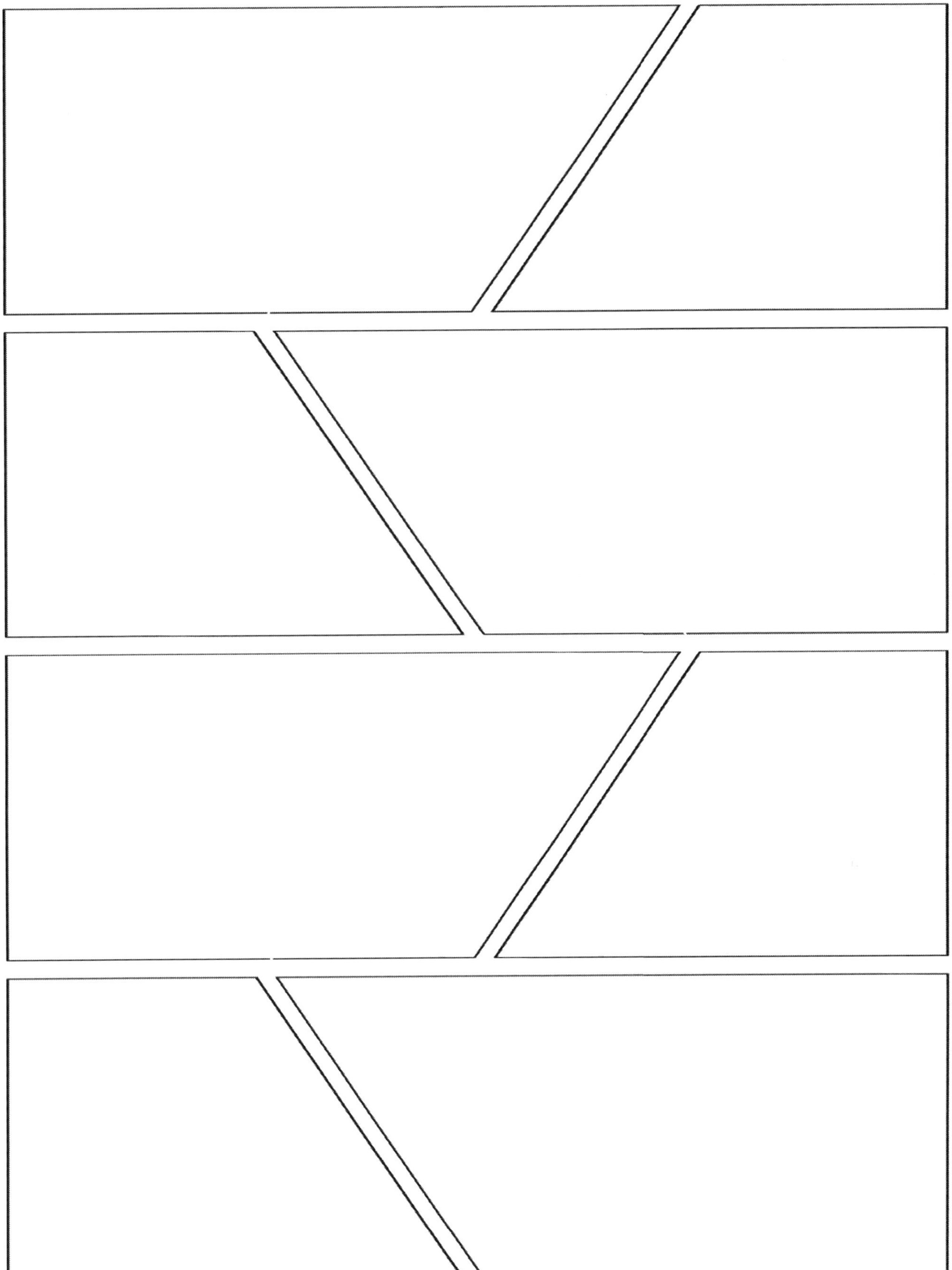

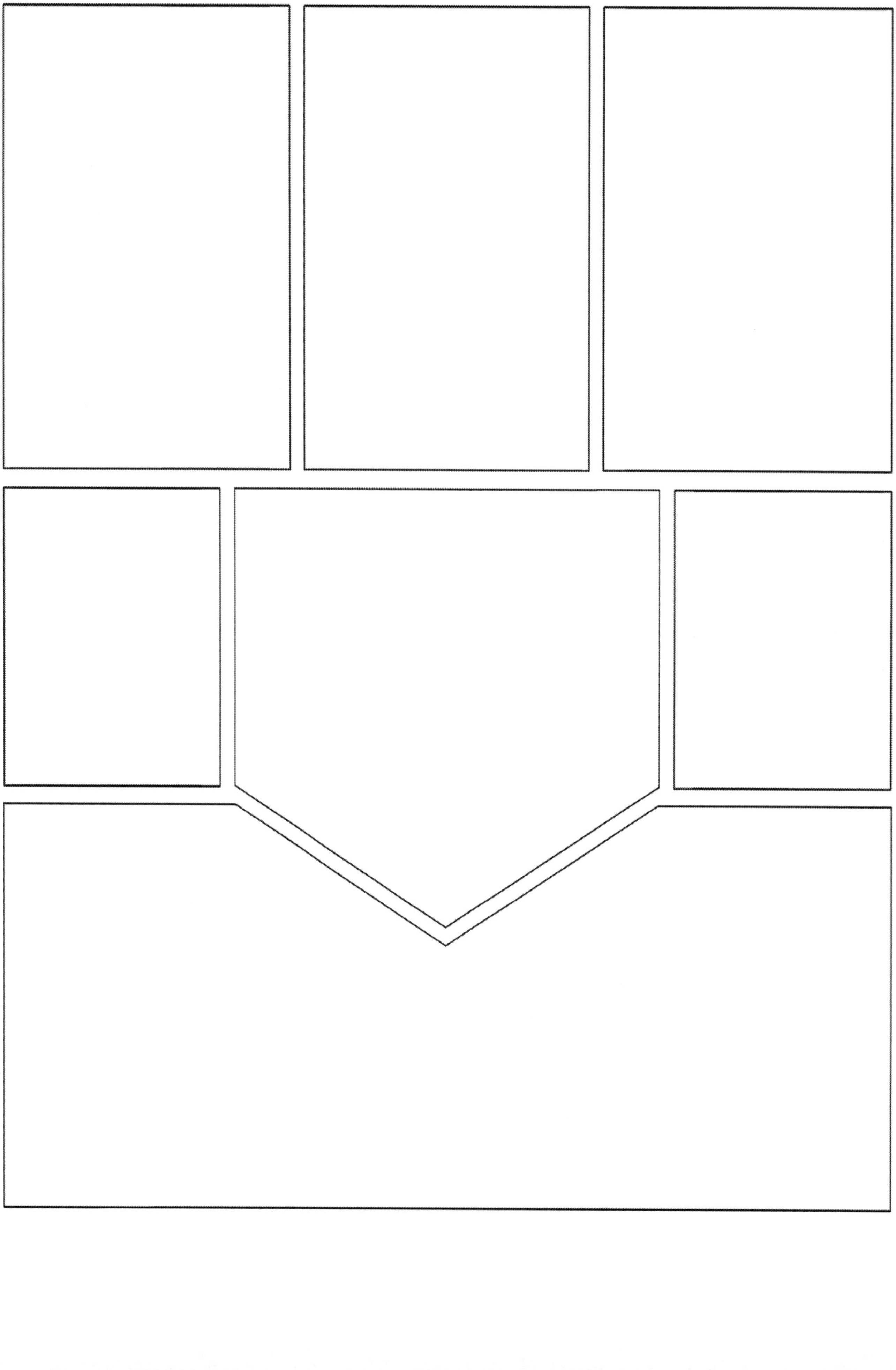

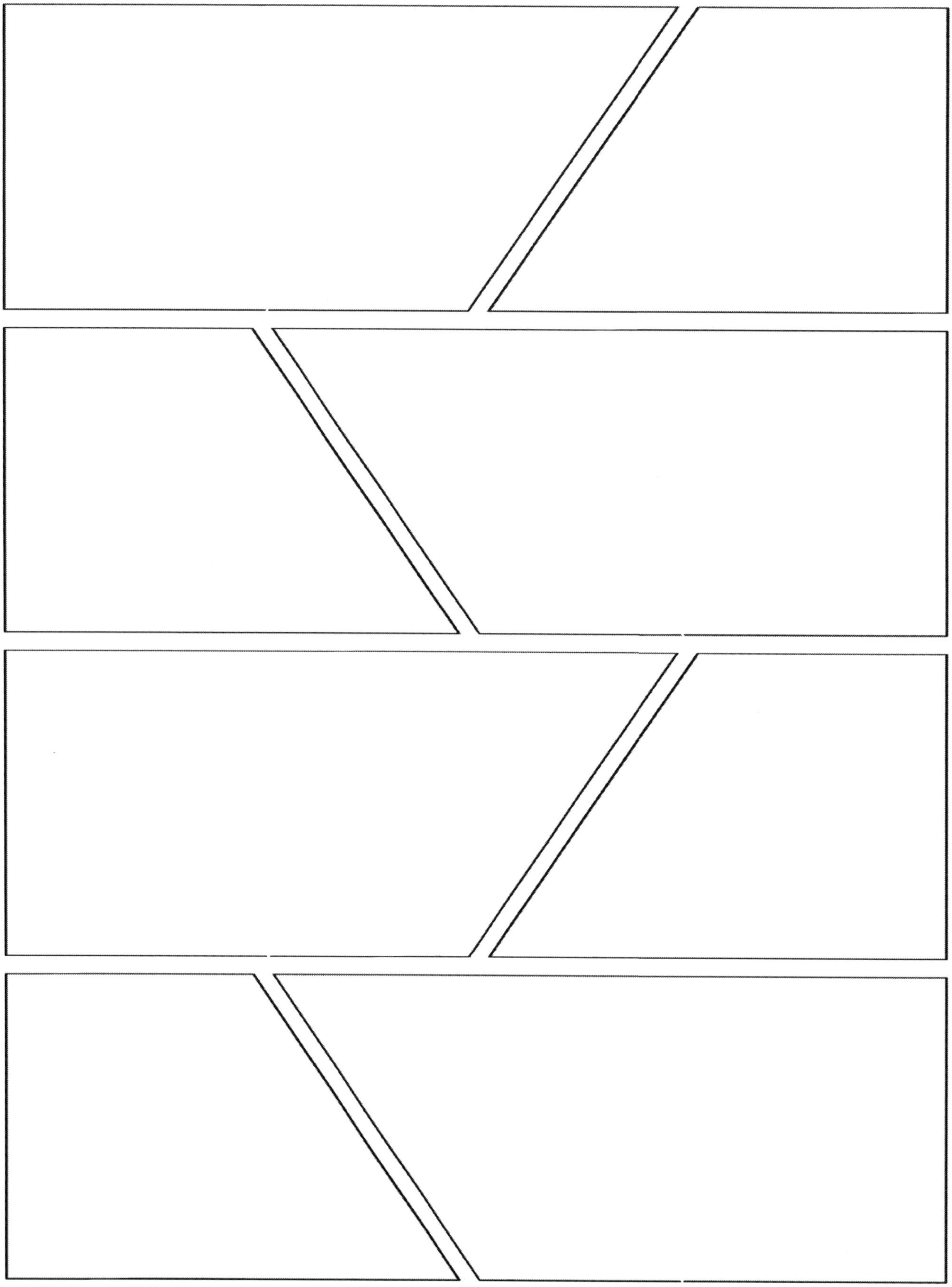

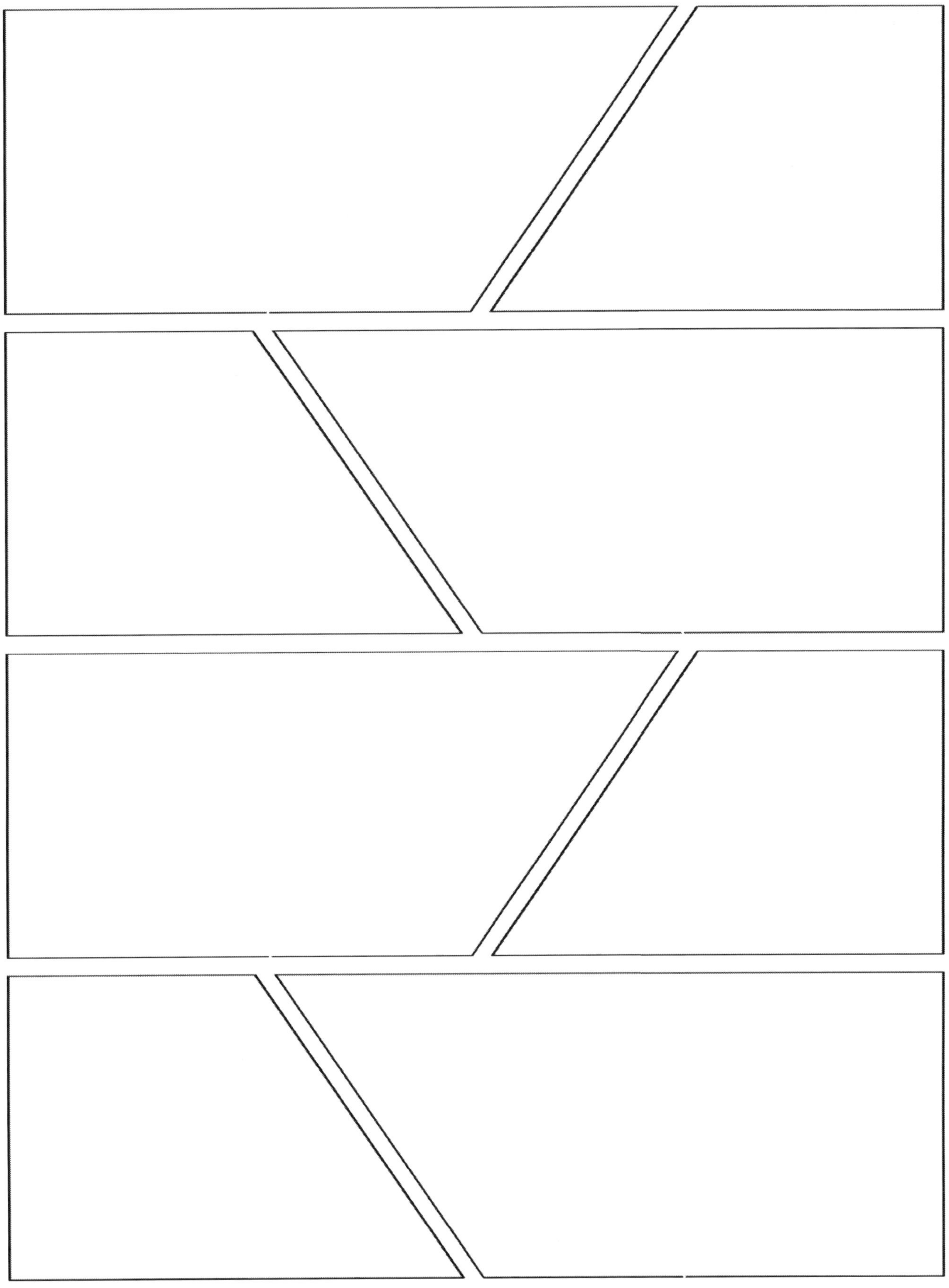

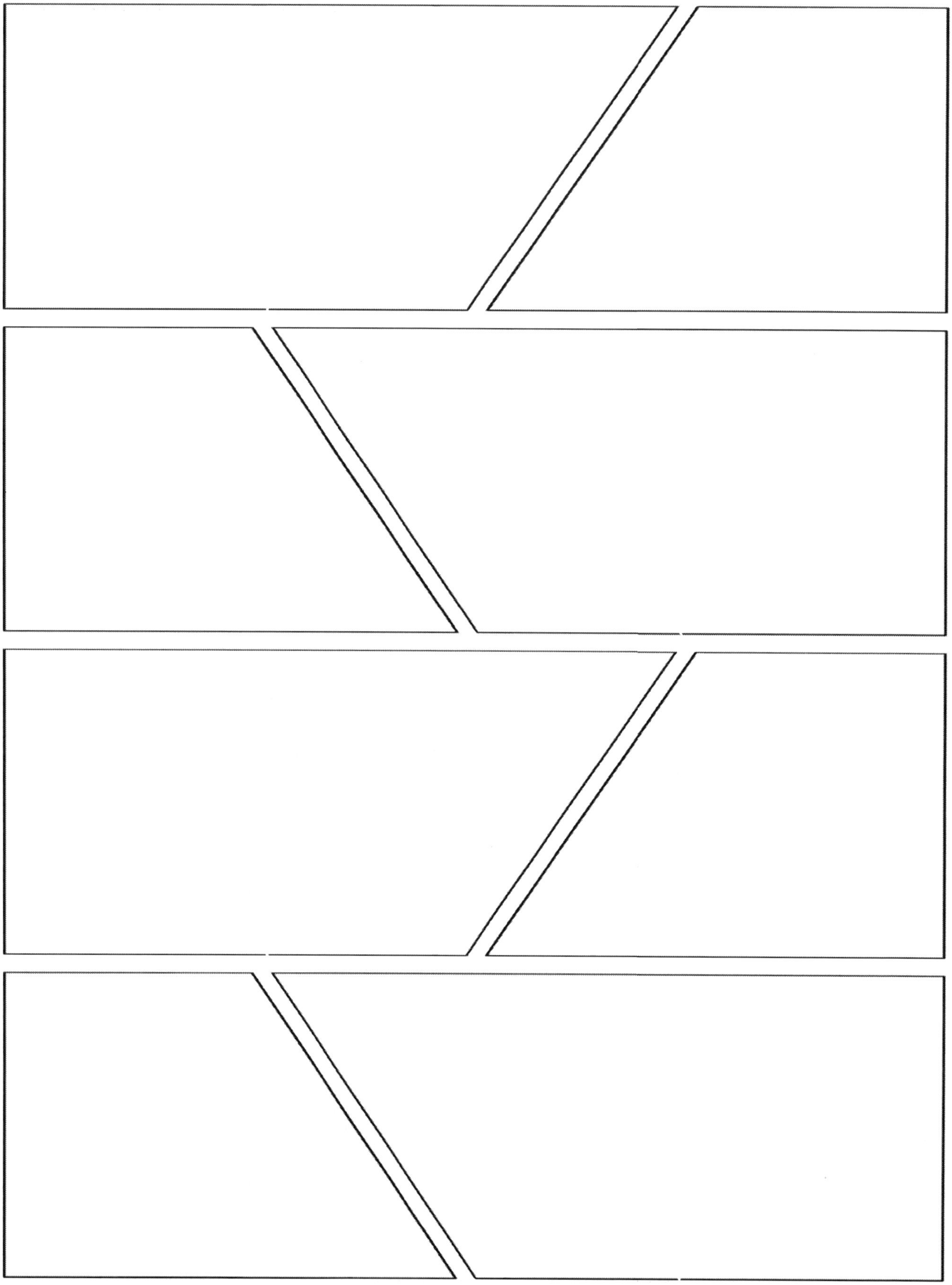

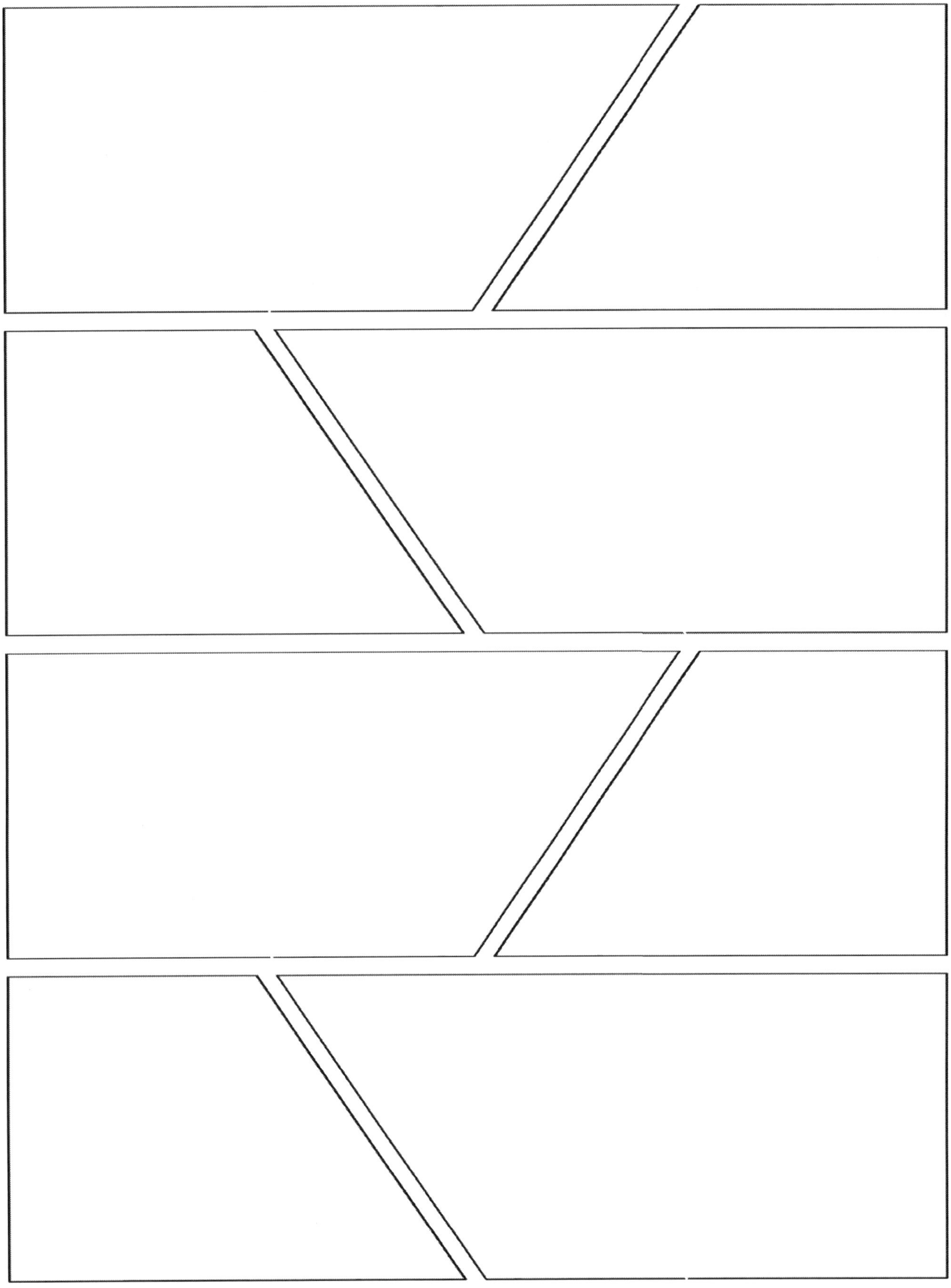

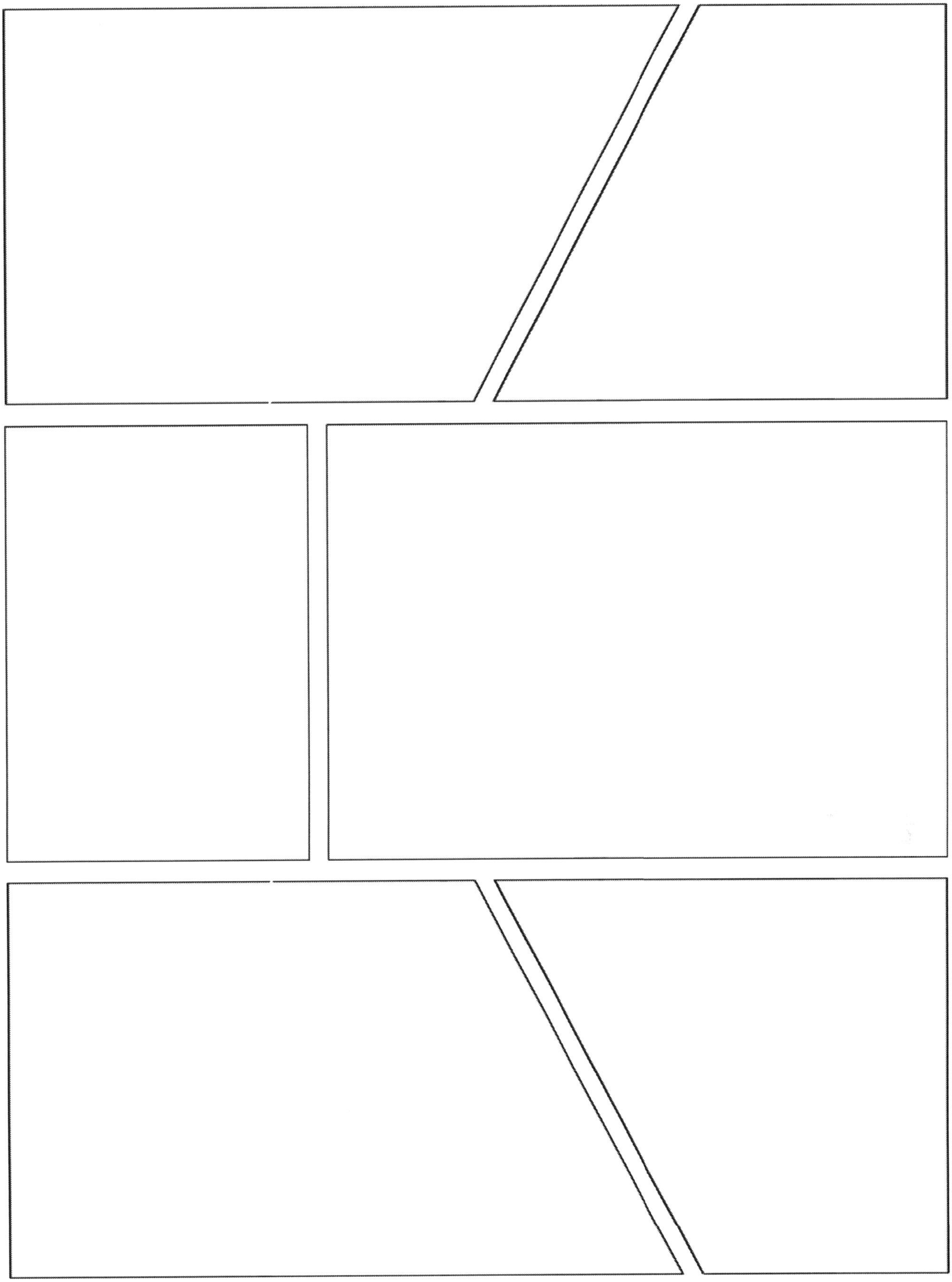

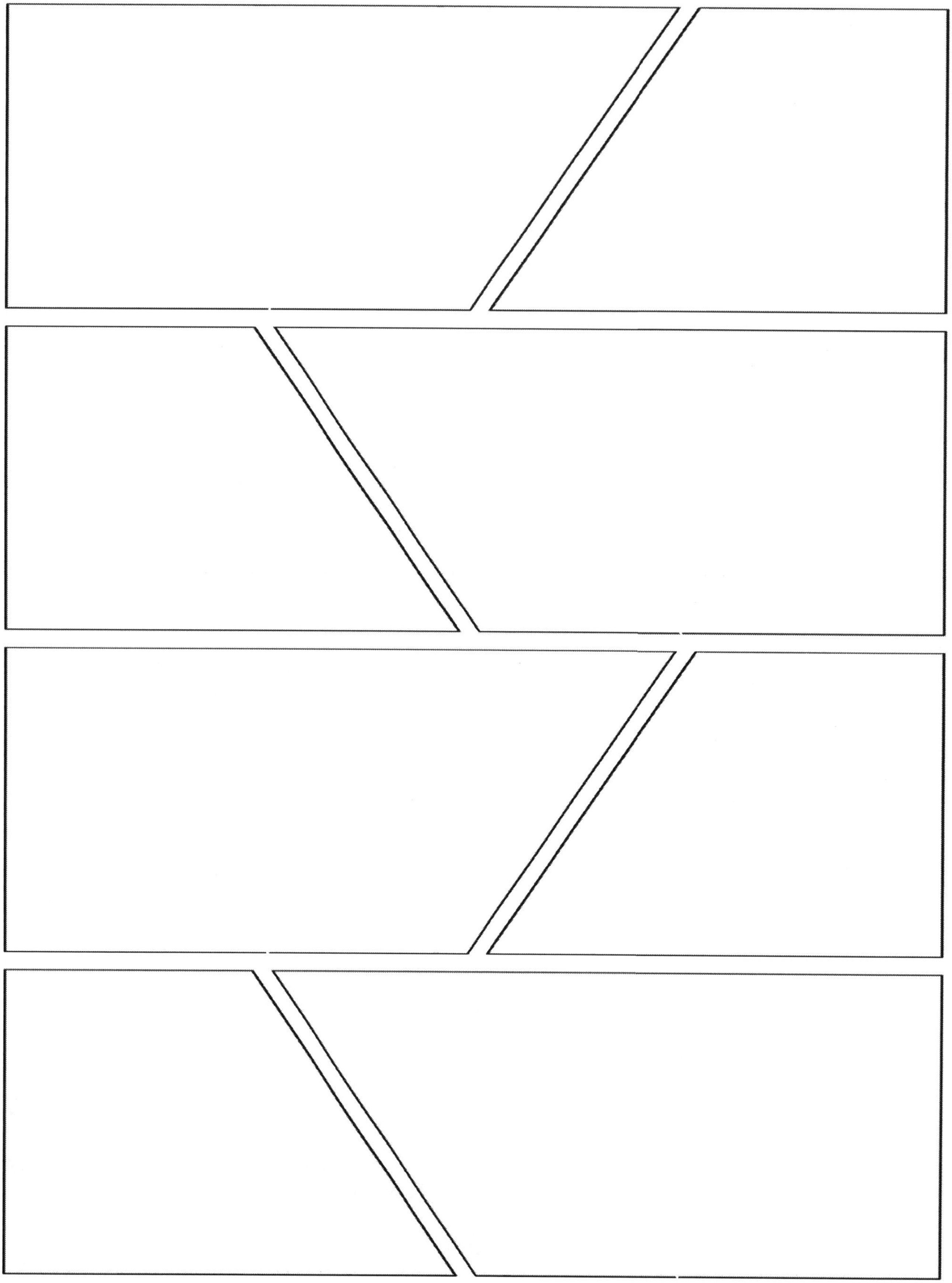

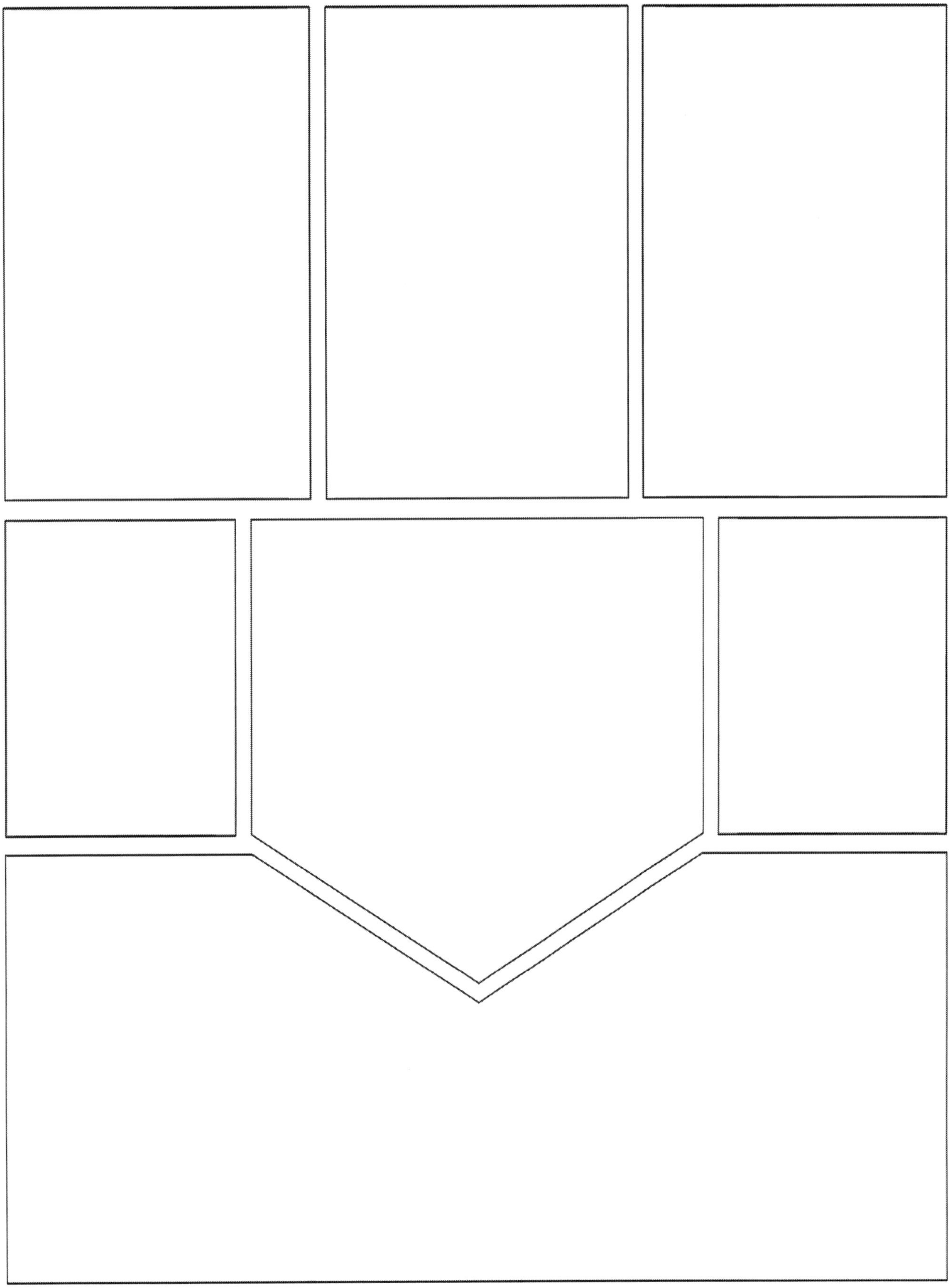

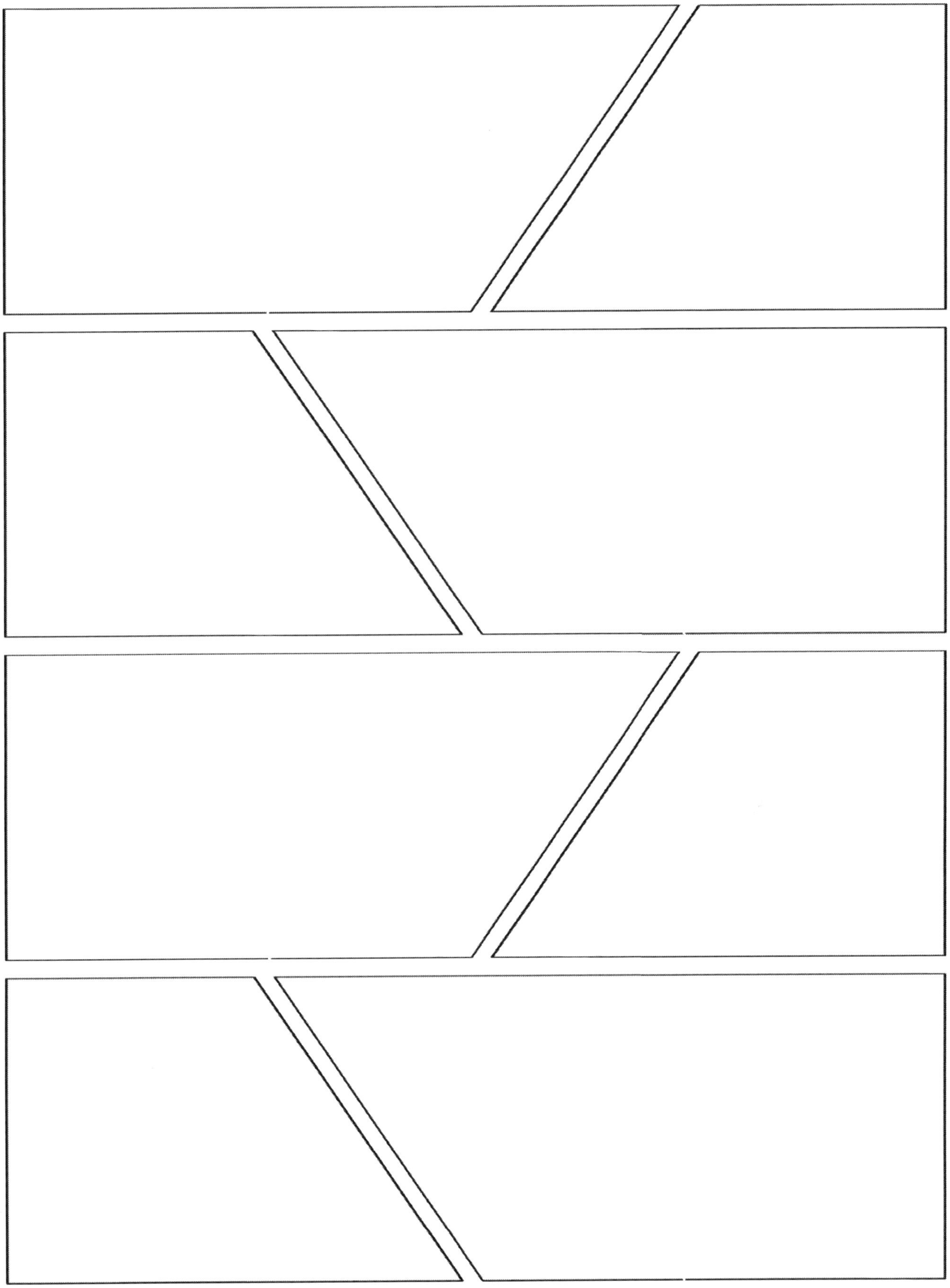

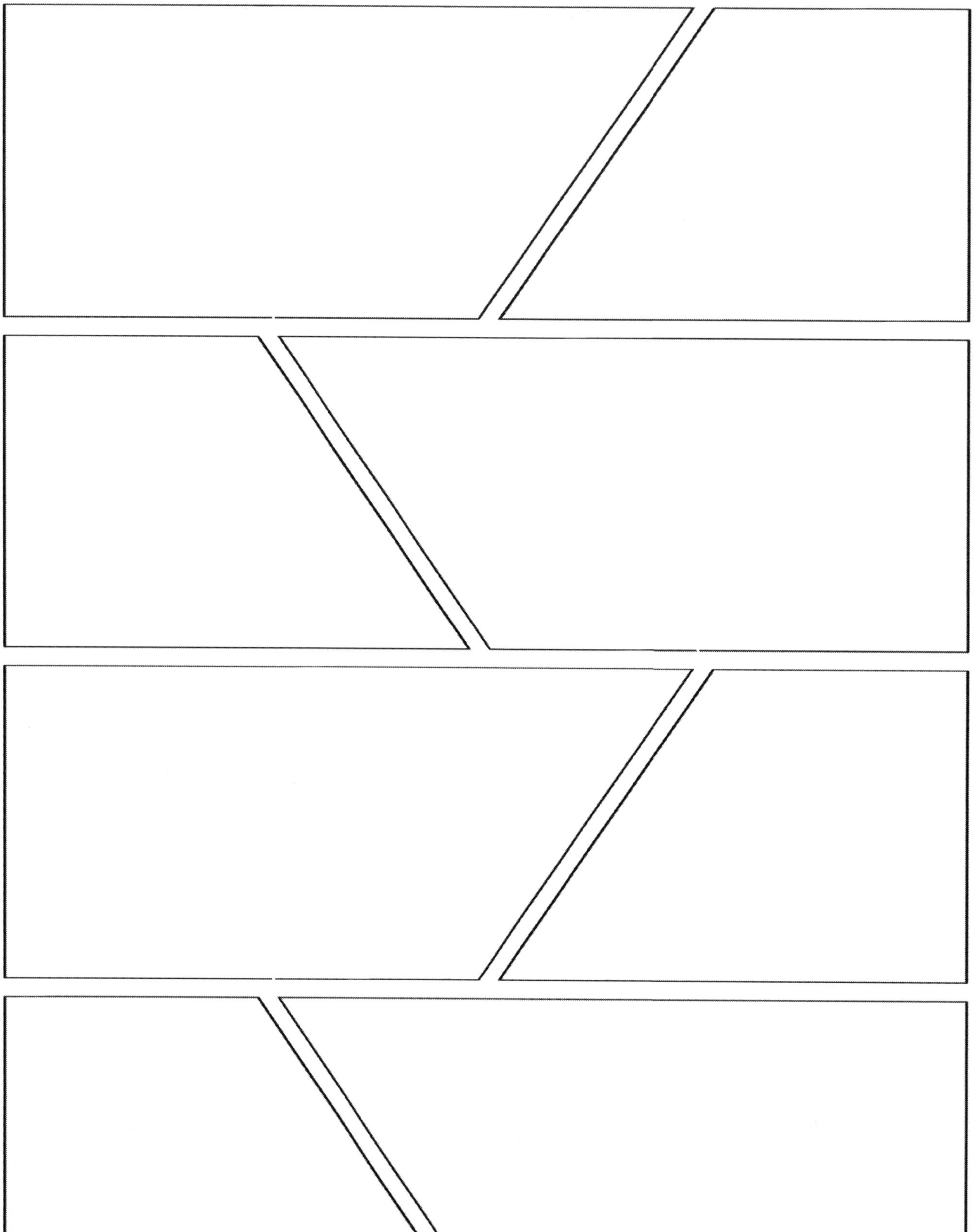

Made in the USA
Monee, IL
10 December 2019

18293674R00077